Life Changing
Prayers

9/25/2016

To Jane Simonds

May God bless
you

AUDREY A. ADDI-MCNEIL

Love

Audrey Addi-McNeil

ISBN: 148182788X
ISBN-13: 978-1481827881

Library of Congress Control Number: 2012924296
CreateSpace Independent Publishing Platform
North Charleston, South Carolina

Acknowledgments

I extend my heartfelt thanks to all those who have prayed with me, believed in me, and guided me in writing this book, *Life-Changing Prayers*. Special thanks to Sister Pricilla Rupoka from Bristol, Connecticut, Heritage Pentecostal Church, for typing a part of this manuscript and praying along with me during my recent illness. To Dr. George and Jireta Peart for encouraging me throughout this journey. To Pastor McDonald, Sister Debbie McDonald, and the church family from Heritage Pentecostal Church for all their love and support during my illness. To Bishop John Paul Diamond, First Lady Roxanne Diamond, and the church family for their constant support and prayers during my illness. To the Cathedral of Faith church family for their support and prayers during my illness. To my Pastor Apostle Darren Phillips and First Lady Valerie Phillips and the Christ United church family for all their love and support during my illness. To Sister Susan Yeskie for all her kindness and prayers and for caring for my home while I am away. To my wonderful grandson, Devonte Brown, for typing a portion of the manuscript. To Sister Carmen Clarke for helping take care of me during my illness. To Reverend Pleasant McGowan, Sister Mal Palmer, and my dear friend, Barbara Mayers, for all their love and support during my illness. To Rabbi and Roslyn Epstein for their constant love and support. To my neighbor, Lolita Teague, who stayed with me and helped me through my illness.

MAY GOD CONTINUE TO BLESS YOU ALL.

Dedication

I would like to dedicate this book, *Life-Changing Prayers*, to my wonderful husband, Dr. Barry McNeil, who has been a true friend to me. Without his love and guidance, I would not have been successful in writing this book. He stood with me in spite of all my challenges. He is my rock. He is my true love. I thank him for praying along with me when I was not able to put my thoughts together during my pain and suffering after my surgery in May 2012. He reminded me that I can accomplish whatever I set my mind to do. I thank him for all the laughter we've shared and the walks we've enjoyed.

I also dedicate this book to the following people:

My parents, the late Martha Ann Rubie and Harold Rubie

My daughter, Claudette Brown, and my son-in-law,
Norman Brown

My wonderful grandson, Dovante Brown

My sisters, Gloria Shaw and Esther Rubie, and their families

My deceased sister, Geneive Chisholm, who died in July 2011

My brothers, John Rubie and Icah Clarke, and their families

The Rubie family and the Nugent family

Mildred Mullings and John Mullings

My sister-in-law, Vivian Parks, and her husband, Robbie Parks

Uncle Bill Graham and his family

TO ALL OF MY FRIENDS

Foreword

Life has a way of presenting some of the most rewarding and challenging experiences that leave us striving for more or just simply wanting to give up. It is in these times that prayer becomes a pivotal part of a person's life. It is our way of intimately sharing our deepest thoughts and feelings with God. Prayer gives us a chance to give thanks for all of God's many blessings, for the wonderful people in our lives, and for our community. It also provides us the opportunity to make our petitions known to God when we face everyday struggles, sickness, and disappointments. Prayer is a powerful tool, but sadly, not many people understand how to pray. They find themselves being repetitive and not being able to stay focused when they go to God in prayer.

In *Life-Changing Prayers*, Audrey Addi-McNeil uses her passion for prayer to help people connect with God and experience His peace, grace, and mercy to see their needs met. You will be drawn in by her spiritual boldness and caring spirit as you read this book. She has a sincere love for prayer, has prayed for many people (including strangers), and has heard testimonies as a result of her prayers. Audrey shares her knowledge of the Bible and the way to pray because there are times in life when most people don't know what to do or how to pray. It is in those times that readers will be able to find their specific need, pray the prayer, and see God perform miracles in their lives.

I am privileged to have Audrey Addi-McNeil cover my family in prayer and share her love of God with us. I encourage you to keep this book close and use it often. You may not have the opportunity to meet her personally, but once you began to read the prayers, I am certain that you will have found your newest friend.

Minister Yolanda Dupree

Table of Contents

CHAPTER 1

Prayer for Forgiveness

When you are faced with unkindness, you must remember that Jesus is the author of forgiveness. He wants us to come to Him and spend time seeking His guidance. Jesus, loving Savior, please help us understand how to forgive those who hurt us time and time again. You have asked your Heavenly Father to forgive us because we don't understand life's daily struggles. We need your grace and wisdom to forgive others just as you have forgiven us.

Thank you, dear Lord, for the gift of forgiveness. Amen.

Scripture reading: Acts 26:18, Col. 1:14

CHAPTER 2

Prayer for Holiness

ithout holiness, it is impossible to please God. Holiness is a part of God's standard for living a peaceful life in this troubled world.

Father, we pray that you will cleanse our lives from sin and give us renewed hope so that we may live a holy life that will be pleasing to you. You have made us in your own image. Because you are holy, we must be holy to walk with you here on earth. We are not worthy of your love and peace, but we come to you with a broken heart that you alone can cleanse. Please help us to live in holiness until you come again.

Thank you, dear Lord, for helping us live in holiness. Amen.

Scripture reading: 1 Chron. 16:29, Ps. 29:2, Isa. 35:8, Zech. 14:20, Rom. 14:20, 2 Cor. 7:1

CHAPTER 3
Prayer for Peace

ord, I am asking you to bring peace to this troubled world. All around our streets and neighborhoods, we can see anger and hopelessness. The only hope that we have is in you, dear Lord. If you don't come to our rescue, we will all fail and lose our way. We need peace instead of wars, and we also need peace to have a brighter tomorrow. Give us peace in the midst of turmoil each and every day. You are the God of peace. When your son, Jesus, left this world, he prayed that we would have peace. Today, we pray for peace all around the world. We pray that our children will learn peace at home so when they move away into other communities, they will live peacefully.

Thank you, dear Lord, for granting us peace. Amen.

Scripture reading: Num. 6:26, Ps. 34:14, Ps. 122:6, Isa. 9:6, Isa. 26:3, Luke 2:29, Gal. 5:22

CHAPTER 4

Prayer for the Four Corners of the Earth

Father God, this is a brand-new day that you have allowed us to see. This is a day that we have never seen before. We come to you with a new heart for souls that live in the east, west, north, and south. These are the four corners of the earth. We don't know everyone who is hurting because of sickness and despair, but you know. We pray that you will send deliverance right now and set them free. I pray that those who cannot make up their minds to serve you will open their hearts to new beginnings. The prayer of our hearts is that you will come down and visit your people once more, and when we get to glory, we will see all of God's people marching in from the four corners of the earth.

Thank you, dear Lord, for hearing and answering this humble prayer. Amen.

Scripture reading: Job 38:4, Ps. 24:1, Ps. 33:5, Eccles. 1:4, Isa. 6:3, Isa. 66:1, 1 Cor. 10:28

CHAPTER 5

Prayer for Love

Loving Father, you are a God of love. You said in your word that without love, it is impossible to please you. We are asking you to send your love down from heaven above upon your children everywhere in this world. Let our hearts and minds be open and receptive to your warm embrace. Your love brings joy and peace when your name is mentioned. Without your love, mankind will remain unfulfilled. Your love is like sunshine when darkness surrounds us. Sweet heavenly Father, please send your precious love so that the world will see more of you.

We thank you, dear Lord, for love. Amen.

Scripture reading: Lev. 19:18, Deut. 6:5, Ps. 119:97, Ps. 145:20, Jer. 31:3, Matt. 5:44

CHAPTER 6

Prayer for Hope

Heavenly Father, we are asking you to give us hope when everything around us seems hopeless. We are faced with uncertainties in our homes, workplaces, and even in our neighborhoods. People are losing their homes, jobs, and even their money is taken from them because of greed. Lord, help us hold onto the hope of your coming. We are reminded in your holy word that we must call upon you, and you will never leave us alone. In Psalm 39:7, King David said, "And now Lord, what wait I for? My hope is in the Lord.". . Yes, Lord, our lives are in your hands, and you can fix all of our problems when we call upon your holy name.

We thank you, dear Lord, for hope. Amen.

Scripture reading: Ps. 31:24, Ps. 42:5, Jer. 14:8, Lam. 3:26, Ezek. 9:12, Rom. 5:4, 1 Cor. 13:13, Gal. 5:5

CHAPTER 7

Prayer for Strength

In Psalm 27:1, King David said, "The Lord is the strength of my life; of whom I shall be afraid?". . Lord, we come before you in need of inner strength. There are times when we are faced with life's temptations and don't know what to do, but we know your strength can help us through our hard times. Please look down from heaven and bless us this day and throughout eternity. Help us read your word daily and walk in your footsteps as we travel along life's pathway. In Isaiah 40:29, the prophet Isaiah said, "But they that wait upon the Lord shall renew their strength.". . We are depending on you to take us through each and every day. We pray for continued strength in all our lives.

We give thanks, dear Lord, for giving us strength. Amen.

Scripture reading: Exod. 15:2, Job 12:13, Ps. 18:32, Ps. 27:1, Ps. 28:7, Ps. 46:1, Ps. 96:6

CHAPTER 8

Prayer for Those Who Are Suffering

Heavenly Father, the world is faced with suffering all around us. Today, we pray that you will shield us from suffering. Many people are suffering from pain all over their bodies; some are suffering from a lack of food and shelter. You alone, Lord, can rescue us from all of life's suffering. Please lighten our burdens during our suffering. Help us take courage from Job. Even though he was experiencing suffering all over his body, he held onto faith without wavering. Lord, I am convinced that you will give us grace to endure all that we face.

Thank you, dear Lord, for hearing and answering our prayer. Amen.

Scripture reading: Job 3:1, Rom. 8:18, Heb. 2:10

CHAPTER 9

Prayer for Patience

Most heavenly Father, we come before you today asking you to give us more patience. Your people are faced with all kinds of disturbances as we travel on our journeys. We need your guiding hands to embrace us as we move from place to place. You alone can protect us from unseen disasters. Our lives will not be secured unless we seek to have more patience with each other. Give us patience with our children, our friends, our family, and all those with whom we come in contact.

Thank you, heavenly Father, for being patient with us, even though we do not deserve your blessings. Amen.

Scripture reading: Matt. 18:29, Luke 8:15, Rom. 5:3, 1 Tim. 6:11, Heb. 12:1, James 1:3

CHAPTER 10

Prayer for Finances

Dear heavenly Father, people are faced with financial difficulties all over the world. You promised in your word that you will supply all our needs according to your riches in glory. When we look to you by faith, we will never be in need. King David said in Psalm 23:1, "The Lord is my shepherd, I shall not want." Please continue to give us wisdom on how to spend our money and live within our means. You are the giver of wealth and by faith; I believe you can restore our finances if we continue to pray.

Thank you, dear Lord, for wisdom in handling our finances. Amen.

Scripture reading: Eccles. 10:19

CHAPTER 11

Prayer for My Neighbors

Most gracious, loving Father, I come to you on behalf of my neighbors. Neighbors are special in your plan. You reminded Moses on Mount Sinai that we should not be covetous toward our neighbors. I pray for all my neighbors. Give them peace and love for each other. Save them from their sins and make them ready for your kingdom. Bless all my neighbors with health, wealth, joy, and happiness.

Thank you, dear Lord, for hearing and answering our prayers. Amen.

Scripture reading: Exod. 20:16–17, Lev. 19:13–20, Prov. 27:10, Matt. 19:19, Matt. 22:39, Luke 10:29

CHAPTER 12

Prayer for Godly Friends

Lord, I pray that you will send godly people into our lives who would want to be our friends. So many times we are in need of friends who offer solace when we are burdened. However, unless such a friend is a believer in the word, our friendship will fail. Proverbs 18:24 states, "A man that hath friends must show himself friendly, and there is a friend that sticketh closer than a brother." Lord, you are the best friend anyone could have. I pray that all my friends will seek you more so that they can be friends in need and friends in deed through Jesus's precious blood.

Thank you, dear Lord, for godly friends. Amen.

Scripture reading: Prov. 17:17, Prov. 18–24, John 15:13, James 2:23, James 4:4.

CHAPTER 13

Prayer for Children in Prison

Dear heavenly Father, many children are locked up in prison because of various circumstances. Some are in prison for things they did not do. Some have committed crimes for which our society will never forgive them, but you love them in spite of their sins. Please have mercy on these children and help them learn more about your grace while they are confined in prison. Send someone to minister your living word to them so that their lives will be changed from wrong to right. Precious Lord, keep them safe until their sentences are over.

Thank you, dear Lord, for hearing and answering this prayer in Jesus's name. Amen.

Scripture reading: Prov. 27:6, Col. 3:20, Eph. 1:5

CHAPTER 14

Prayer for Parents in Prison

Father, our prisons are filled with parents all over the world. We need to hear from you so that this breakdown in our society can cease. We must pray for children who are hurting because of the lack of care from their parents. Unless we help these parents, we will continue to have delinquent children who suffer from a lack of a proper family life. You are the giver of Life. You said if any man thirsts, he should come and drink of the water of life. Parents need guidance that can be found only in your words. Father, please send someone to share the good news of salvation while these parents are locked up in prison.

Thank you, Lord, for hearing and answering this prayer in Jesus's name. Amen.

Scripture reading: 2 Cor. 12:14

CHAPTER 15

Prayer for Food

Lord our God, in your word you told the story about feeding the multitude. Without food, we cannot function the way we are supposed to. This day we pray that you will feed those all over the world who don't have food. Help each of us share with those who are in need. When I think of the children who don't have food, it reminds me of your graciousness to the prophet Elijah. You supplied his needs even during the famine. If you showed compassion on Elijah, I know you will show compassion today on the people of the world. I believe you can make the dry land yield a crop for a time of need in this world.

Thank you, Lord, for providing food for people all over the world. Amen.

Scripture reading: Gen. 3:6, Ps. 78:25, 1 Pet. 5:2, Rom. 12:20

CHAPTER 16

Prayer for Shelter

Jesus, you are our shelter in the time of a storm. When Peter was afraid during the storm, you commanded the wind to be still. You can do all things. Many people don't have anywhere to live; some are sleeping out in the cold. We need you, dear Lord, to make it possible for everyone to have shelter from the wind, the rain, and the snow. Dear Lord, please supply all of your children's needs.

In the Garden of Eden, after Adam and Eve sinned, you showed compassion and clothed them. I am reminded of your love for all mankind. Poor people are suffering all around the world because of a lack of shelter. Today, Lord, we humbly ask you to provide shelter for those who are in need of a home.

Thank you, dear Lord, for hearing and answering this prayer. Amen.

Scripture reading: Prov. 11:29, Gen. 3:1–3

CHAPTER 17

Prayer for Clothing

Lord, so many people don't have clothing to wear to protect themselves from the elements. I pray that you will send someone to fill these needs for all those who need clothing. In Exodus 28:40, you commanded that Aaron's sons should have coats, girdles, and bonnets for glory and beauty. You will never change in your doings. Your people are suffering here on earth for basic needs. Please, dear Father, give people jobs so that they can buy the clothing necessary for them to go into your house of worship and give you praise. You promised that you will withhold nothing good from your children. Please help those who have much to share with those who are in need.

Thank you, Lord, for hearing and answering this prayer. Amen.

Scripture reading: Exod. 28:40, Gen. 3:7, Matt. 5:40, 2 Tim. 4:13, Acts 21:11, Luke 20:46

CHAPTER 18

Prayer for Safe Communities

Father, many communities are being destroyed because of various crimes. Families are not safe as they walk or drive around. Children sometimes bear the brunt of man's cruelty. If you don't come to our rescue, we will fail. I am asking you to safeguard all communities so that we will have peace, joy, and love one another. Help us look out for each other on a daily basis and share the good news of your coming. I pray that communities will pray together and seek constant guidance from your word. Please send your angels to guard and protect communities all over the world.

Thank you, dear Lord, for hearing and answering this prayer in Jesus's name. Amen.

Scripture reading: 2 Tim. 3:16–17

CHAPTER 19

Prayer for a Car

Lord, we are living in a world in which transportation is necessary to get to and from most jobs. Many people cannot work because they lack transportation. This prayer is made today on their behalf. Lord, please help those who need a car to be successful in their search. Help your children dear Lord, to give you thanks always for all the good that you have done for them. Bless those who are always eager to share a ride for those in need of transportation. When you were here on earth, you traveled by boat, donkey, and even walked. Lord, times have changed since you walked the earth, so please grant this request for all of those who are in need of a car today.

Dear Lord, we give you praise for hearing this prayer in Jesus's name. Amen.

CHAPTER 20
Prayer to Get Out of Debt

Loving God, maker of mankind and the universe, I pray that you will release all your people who are burdened with needless debt. The world once owed a debt that we could not pay, and it was then that you went to the cross and freed us from the debt of sin. We thank you for freeing us from the debt of sin. Many people are depressed and sometimes suicidal because of the weight of their debts. Please give us wisdom to live within our means. Help us change the way we value money, and teach us to save a little for tomorrow so that our financial needs will be met.

We thank you, dear Lord, for guidance in our struggle to get out of debt. Amen.

Scripture reading: Matt. 6:9–15, Rom. 1:14–17, Rom. 6:7–12

CHAPTER 21

Prayer for Children

Lord, you said in your word, in John 14:14, that if we ask anything in your name, you will give it to us. Many women all over the land are in need of children. Please open their wombs and bless them with their hearts' desire. Help these women to be good mothers when they have children because children are special in so many ways; they bring joy to our lonely hearts. Those who need children sometimes pay large amounts of money to adopt children because they are not able to give birth on their own. You alone know the hearts of these women. I believe you will show love and mercy to women around the world who need to have children. Let your blessings flow upon these women who are crying out for children of their own.

Thank you, dear Lord, for the gift of children. Amen.

Scripture reading: Ps. 127: 3–5, Matt. 7:7, John 14:14, Eph. 3:20, Eph. 6:1–3

CHAPTER 22

Prayer for Grandchildren

ord, many parents have raised their children and now wish to have grandchildren to perpetuate their bloodline.. Make it possible for these mothers and fathers to be blessed with grandchildren so that future generations will exist. Most grandchildren show unconditional love to their grandparents. I thank you, Lord, for my own grandson, Dovante Gray Brown, who makes my heart joyful. Please continue to watch over these grandchildren you have given us. Help them study the word of God on a daily basis until you come to claim this world for your kingdom in heaven.

Thank you, dear Lord, for the great gift of grandchildren. Amen.

Scripture reading: Ps. 127:3–5, Matt. 1:1–25, Acts 7:8–15, 2 Tim. 1:5–7

CHAPTER 23

Prayer for a Job

Lord, this current economy has caused so many people to lose their jobs. Many people want to work but can't find a job. Unless you help these people find a source of employment, they will suffer both financially and emotionally. People have lost their homes because of a lack of funds. If you don't help them, it will be difficult for them to live in this troubled world. You said, "Whatsoever our hands findeth to do, do it with thy might;" Lord, we ask you to help your people to trust you, in spite of their lack of jobs. You are the source of our being and the giver of all good jobs. Lord, we look to you for all our provision, so please help those in need of a job to find one.

Thank you, dear Lord, for providing us with jobs. Amen.

Scripture reading: Eccles. 9:10, Ps. 8:3, Ps. 8:6, Isa. 64:8, John 9:4, 1 Cor. 3:8, 1 Cor. 4:12, 1 Tim. 5:8

CHAPTER 24

Prayer for Peaceful Coworkers

ord, everyone must work together for the common good of the land. People cannot do everything in this world by themselves. We need each other to survive. When you placed Adam in the Garden of Eden, you saw that he needed company and created Eve to support him. We need good coworkers so that we can function on the job from day to day. Help us to be peaceful with each other. Help us pray for one another. No matter what the task, we can make it when we support each other's work. This is the prayer of my heart for all coworkers around the world.

Thank you, dear Lord, for peaceful coworkers. Amen.

Scripture reading: Acts 10:34–35, Gal. 5:14, Gal. 6:10, Titus 3:8, Titus 3:14, Heb. 13:21

CHAPTER 25

Prayer for Favors on the Job

Great Heavenly Father, I come to you with a special request to grant your children favor on our jobs. Lord, please grant divine favors to your children so that we can find peace and happiness on the job. We are thankful for all favors, and all things are possible with you. Some jobs are more secure than others because of your undoubting favors. Please help your people who need work find jobs that will meet their needs so that they can care for their families and support your work here on earth. You showed favor to Joseph when he was put in charge of Pharaoh's household. I am confident that you can grant favors to those who ask your blessing this day. Help all those who are working to do the best job possible so that they will maintain favors from their bosses all around the world.

Thank you, dear Lord, for favors on the job. Amen.

Scripture reading: Mark 9:23

CHAPTER 26

Prayer for Our Government

Lord, you put the government in charge of our country and ordered mankind to follow directions for the common good of the people. When you started this world, things were done in order; you are a God of order. If the government were not in place to provide leadership, the land would have constant unrest. We pray this day that the government will help bring order and stability to our land. Help government leaders understand their duties to your people and help them solve problems so our nation will follow under the principles that you have ordained in your word. Lord, please help our leaders realize that without your guidance they will not be able to govern your people here on earth. We ask your blessings upon all governments around the world.

Thank you, dear Lord, for watching over our government. Amen.

CHAPTER 27

Prayer for the Land

Heavenly Father, maker of heaven and earth, I come before you today to give thanks for the land you have given us. In your word, you said, "The earth is the Lord's and the fullness thereof." You separated the land from the waters so that mankind would have a safe dwelling place. We thank you for the splendor of the land. We thank you for the food and fresh flowers the land has yielded. We praise your name for the trees that give us shade from the sun. You have also given us various ores and minerals to enrich our lives. You are loving and kind in all you do. Help your people all over the world share space with each other on this land and to live in unity until you come again.

Thank you, dear Lord, for the blessing of this land. Amen.

Scripture reading: Gen. 1:9–12, Gen. 1:29, Ps. 24:1

CHAPTER 28

Prayer for the Animals

Dear Lord, you created various animals from the dawn of creation to enrich our lives. Animals were named by Adam in the Garden of Eden. You have instructed priests and prophets how to care for animals, even in the making of sacrifice unto you. We thank you for all animals on this earth. Without animals, we would not have the nourishment needed for our bodies. Without the animals you provided to take us from place to place, some people would not be able to move around. We thank you, Lord, for animals that help us bear our heavy loads in traveling from place to place. Help us to be kind to all animals; we know you have made them for a purpose.

Thank you, dear Lord, for blessing all animals. Amen.

Scripture reading: Gen. 1:20–25, Gen. 1:30, Gen. 6:19–20

CHAPTER 29

Prayer for Water

Precious Lord, you are the giver of all good gifts. You have given everything to make our lives complete. I am thankful that you have given us water so that we can quench our thirst. Without water, we will not survive on this planet. We thank you for sending rain to flow into rivers and streams so that all crops can grow. Yes, Lord, we also thank you for the water upon the seas that allows ships to sail from place to place to take food to those who are in need. Only you, Lord, can supply our every need.

We thank you, dear Lord, for giving us water every day. Amen.

Scripture reading: Ps. 22:14, Isa. 12:3, Isa. 44:3, Isa. 58:11, Ezek. 36:25, Matt. 3:11, Matt. 10:42, Luke 16: 24

CHAPTER 30

Prayer for Rain

"Our Father, which art in heaven, hallowed be thy name.". Lord, we thank you for your many blessings that you have bestowed upon your children here on earth. Today, we pray for rain upon all those cities that need it. Many cities in this world are experiencing drought. Without your help, your precious people will perish. You have sent rain to the just and the unjust. Help your people serve you in spite of difficult times. Increase our faith, oh, Lord, and help us put our trust in you for all of our needs. You and you only can send rain. Lord, we will continue to give you honor and glory for all you have done.

Lord, we thank you for sending rain upon all cities in need of moisture. Amen.

Scripture reading: Isa. 55:10, Matt. 5:45, Rev. 14:7

CHAPTER 31
Prayer for Knowledge

Most Gracious God, you are the giver of all good gifts. We thank you for the knowledge you have given to your people. I pray that we will use the knowledge you have given us to make this world a safer place to dwell in. Help us share our knowledge for good and not for evil. Many people are seeking knowledge for the wrong reasons. King Solomon prayed to you for an understanding heart to be able to discern between good and bad. You gave him a wise and understanding heart. Lord, we pray that you will equip your people all over the world with the knowledge of peace and love for each other. Having knowledge will help your people plan for the future like Joseph did while he was in Egypt.

We thank you, dear Lord, for granting us the gift of knowledge. Amen.

Scripture reading: Gen. 2:17, 1 Kings 3:9–12, Ps. 19:2, Ps. 139:6, Hosea 4:6, Hab. 2:14, Rom. 3:20, 1 Cor. 8:1, Eph. 3:19

CHAPTER 32

Prayer for Traveling Mercies

As we journey throughout the land, we pray that our heavenly Father will guide our steps and make us safe. Lord, we are living in a mobile world in which traveling is a part of life, but to make our journey safely, we must seek your constant protection. When we travel in our cars, we are always mindful that cars are man-made and sometimes fail. When you guide our journey, we feel safer in our travels. You can see dangers ahead when we cannot see them. Please send your choice angels to guide and protect us as we travel each day. It is comforting to know that you are the keeper of the universe, and you promised to take care of your children. Just as you made a safe passage for the children of Israel as they traveled across the Red Sea, I know you will do the same for all your children who ask for safe traveling in your name.

Thank you, dear Lord, for safe traveling. Amen.

Scripture reading: Gen. 43:1–33, Exod. 3:16–22, Exod. 14:13–31, Acts 9:3, Acts 10:1–26, Acts 18:1–28

CHAPTER 33

Prayer for Rebellious Children

Dear Lord, we are living in a world that is filled with rebellious children. Parents are no longer able to control their children. Some children are abusive to their parents and even to others in our society. Rebellion started a long time ago because of Adam's sin. We pray, Lord, that children will find joy once more in reading your word. Help parents spend time seeking more of your word so that they can raise their children in a godly manner. Help parents speak kind words to their children. You said in Proverbs 22:6 that we must "train up a child in the way he should go,: and when he is old, he will not depart from it." . Some parents need guidance so that they can make good choices in raising their children. Children are our future generation. I am asking you to guide the children with wisdom so that they will become productive citizens in our land.

Thank you, dear Lord, for guiding rebellious children. Amen.

Scripture reading: Num. 14:1–45, Num. 16:1–50, Prov. 22:6

CHAPTER 34

Prayer for Good Friends

Loving father, you know the hearts of mankind. You made us in your own image. I thank you for all my good friends who are in my life. King Solomon said in Proverbs 18:24, "A man that hath friends must show himself friendly,: and there is a friend that sticketh closer than a brother." Help us show love to our friends and kindness as we pass through this land. Sometimes it is hard to find a good friend when we are in need, but if we seek your guidance, you will always guide us to the right person. Let us lift our friends up in prayer daily and encourage them with your word.

Thank you, dear Lord, for giving us good friends. Amen.

Scripture reading: Prov. 17:17, Prov. 18:24, John 15:13, James 2:23

CHAPTER 35
Prayer to Be a Good Parent

salm 8:1 says, "Oh, LORD, our Lord, how excellent is thy name in all the earth!" You have made mankind to be a good steward in all the land. Please help us be good parents to our children. Parents need guidance that only you can give. Please give parents wisdom to seek your will. Parents are special in many ways. Help parents care for their children to the best of their abilities. Without good parents, most children will not survive. We need good parents all over the world to care for their children. Please help parents provide shelter, food, clothing, and much-needed love. Let parents know they must secure a foundation for their children. Good parents will teach their children how to seek your word by example.

I pray an everlasting blessing for all good parents around the world.

Thank you, dear Lord, for helping us to be good parents. Amen.

Scripture reading: Ps. 8:1, Matt. 7:11, Luke 18:29, Rom. 1:30, 2 Cor. 9:8, 2 Cor. 12:14, Eph. 2:10, Eph. 6:14, Phil. 1:6, 2 Tim. 2:7

CHAPTER 36

Prayer for More Love in the Family

Sweet heavenly Father, you created the first family in the Garden of Eden. Families today sometimes don't love one another the way they should. I pray, dear Lord, that you will grant us more love in the family. Please help families all over the world unite in oneness and seek more of your word. I pray that families will forgive one another for past wrongs. Families are special in your sight. If the family will pray together, then they will stay together. Only your presence can help bridge the gap between family members. Please help families share with each other for the common good of the family. Restore joy, peace, and abiding love throughout the land to all families.

Thank you, dear Lord, for providing the gift of love in the family. Amen.

Scripture reading: Gen. 1:27–31, Gen. 2:7–25, Deut. 6:5, Ps. 68:6, John 13:34, John 14:23, John 15:9, John 15:13, Rom. 8:35, Rom. 12:9

CHAPTER 37

Prayer to Read the Word of God Daily

Dear Lord, help us read your word on a daily basis. Reading your word daily will give us strength when we are weak. We need your sustenance to prevent Satan from attacking us. When you were fasting, you reminded Satan in Matthew 4:7 that "It is written again, thou shalt not tempt the Lord thy God.". Without your word, we cannot make it in this troubled world. In Psalm 119:105, King David said, "Thy word is a lamp unto my feet and a light unto my path." Father, when we read your word on a daily basis, we will find joy, peace, love, and forgiveness. Your word is food to our souls. In Matthew 6:9 and 11, you instructed us how to pray: "Our Father, which art in heaven, hallowed be thy name. Give us this day our daily bread….". Father, we thank you for the living word that sustains us from day to day.

Thank you, dear Lord, for the ability to keep reading your word. Amen.

Scripture reading: Ps. 119:105, Prov. 15:26, Eccles. 12:14, Matt. 6:9, Matt. 6:11, Mark 8:38, John 15:7

CHAPTER 38

Prayer for More Knowledge of the Word

"How excellent is thy name in all the earth!" Oh, Lord, you have given your son, Jesus, to save the world from sin. We come before you asking for greater knowledge of your word. Grant us knowledge that will make a difference in our lives. Help your children spend time reading the Bible to gain knowledge that we can pass on to the next generation. When we have knowledge of your word, it will teach us how to live free from sin and treat mankind with love and humility. 2 Peter 3:18 says, "But grow in grace, and in the knowledge of our Lord and Savior Jesus Christ. To him be glory both now and forever.".

Thank you, dear Lord, for giving us the gift of knowledge. Amen.

Scripture reading: Gen. 2:17, Ps. 8:9, Ps. 19:2, Ps. 139:6, Hosea 4:6, Hab. 2:14, Rom. 3:20, 1 Cor. 8:1, Eph. 3:19, 2 Pet. 3:18

CHAPTER 39

Prayer for Compassion

Loving Jesus, you are the master of compassion. When you went to the cross, you showed the ultimate compassion for Adam's fallen race. You gave your all so that men could be free from their sins. I pray that you will give us that same kind of love so that we can treat one another with boundless compassion when in need. You have forgiven us of our sins instead of sending us to hell. We thank you, Lord, for such mercy and grace. When you were on the cross, you said, "Father, forgive them for they know not what they do." You showed compassion for your children here on earth. We thank you for showing love through the stripes you took upon your body. Help us be compassionate to our frail elderly, the poor and needy, orphans, and all of God's people who are in need around the world.

We thank you, dear Lord, for hearing and answering this plea for compassion. Amen.

Scripture reading: Lam. 3:22, Matt. 15:32, Mark 1:41, Luke 15:20, Luke 23:34, 1 Pet. 3:8

CHAPTER 40

Prayer for Gentleness

Dear Lord, Paul declared in Galatians 5:22–23, "But the fruit of the Spirit is love, joy, peace, longsuffering, gentleness, goodness, faith, meekness, temperance: against such there is no law." We thank you, Lord, for all of these gifts that you have given to us that we can share with others. When we follow your commandments, we will never stray from your word. We pray that gentleness will evolve within each of us on a daily basis. We are placed on earth to do good toward each other. Without reading and studying your word, we will not be able to do your will here on earth. We must bear the fruits of the Spirit so that we can be counted worthy when you return for your chosen people. Help us, dear Lord, follow in your footsteps. Everywhere you went while here on earth, you performed good deeds. If we practice gentleness, we will empower the whole world, one person at a time.

Thank you, dear Lord, for the gift of gentleness. Amen.

Scripture reading: 2 Cor. 10:1, Gal. 5:22–23

CHAPTER 41

Prayer for Mercy

ear Lord, you are the giver of all things. You show mercy upon your people even when we don't deserve it. Your people have rebelled against your word, but you still send the rain and sunshine so that we can survive here on earth. You are merciful in all your doings. We thank you, Lord, for your loving-kindness and your tender mercies. Moses said in Exodus 34:6, "The LORD, the LORD God, merciful and gracious, longsuffering, and abundant in goodness and truth." Even though we are unfaithful, you still show us mercy. We all are destined for hell, but you went to the cross to give us a second chance. We thank you for your mercy and grace. Help your people show mercy to each other as we travel along life's pathway. King David said in Psalm 103:8, "The Lord is merciful and gracious, slow to anger, and plenteous in mercy." Please do not send your wrath upon your children. Help us pray and seek more of you so that we will stay ready until you come.

Thank you, dear Lord, for bestowing your mercy upon us. Amen.

Scripture reading: Exod. 34:7, Ps. 23:6, Ps. 101:1, Ps. 103:8, Hosea 6:6, Hosea 14:3, Mic. 6:8, Luke 1:50

CHAPTER 42

Prayer for Good Gifts

Lord, you have bestowed various gifts upon your children. Help us walk in the gift of our calling. You have provided teaching, preaching, and witnessing. Whatever our gifts may be, may we find comfort in your word so that we can work to the best of our abilities. Gifts are given according to our needs. Some people are not able to sing, but they can pray. Help everyone focus on their strengths instead of their weaknesses. Lord, your gifts are everlasting; all good and perfect gifts cometh from above. You are the giver of all good things. Matthew 7:11 says, "If ye then, being evil, know how to give good gifts unto your children, how much more shall your Father which is in heaven give good things to them that ask him?" Help us, Lord, to turn away from our sins and walk in your light. In Romans 6:23, Paul said, "But the gift of God is eternal life through Jesus Christ our Lord."

Thank you, dear Lord, for good gifts. Amen.

Scripture reading: Matt. 7:11, Rom. 6:23, 1 Cor.7:7, Eph. 2:8

CHAPTER 43

Prayer for Good Teachers

Dear Lord, in Matthew 28:19-20, you have commanded your children, "Go ye therefore and teach all nations, baptizing them in the name of the Father, and of the Son, and of the Holy Ghost. Teaching them to observe all things whatsoever I have commanded you: and lo, I am with you always, even unto the end of the world." Your presence will always be with us as we study your word. We are faced with a great dilemma in our world today because we cannot find good teachers to teach our children. Lord, I pray that you will send godly teachers into our schools and churches to declare the living word of God. This will make a difference in our children's lives and help them be obedient in school. We pray that the anointing of the Holy Ghost will empower all teachers as they teach your word. Without good teachers, we will lose the ability to carry out your mission here on earth. Please bless all teachers around the world. Also, help mothers and fathers be good teachers in their homes.

Thank you, dear Lord, for giving us good teachers. Amen.

Scripture reading: Deut. 4:9, Ps. 51:13, Isa. 2:3, Matt. 28:19-20, 1 John 2:27

CHAPTER 44

Prayer for Cheating Spouses

Precious Lord, you have made male and female to commit to each other in the union of marriage. The first marriage started in the Garden of Eden. Today, many marriages are in trouble because of cheating spouses. I pray, Lord, that we will go back to marriage as you established it and follow your commandments. In Paul's writing to the Ephesians, he said, "Husbands, love your wives, even as Christ also loved the church and gave himself for it." In Romans 13:10, Paul also stated, "Love worketh no ill to his neighbor: therefore love is the fulfilling of the law." When spouses forget to read and practice your word, Satan will enter their lives and cause confusion. We must seek guidance on a daily basis by praying for our spouses. If love is lacking, dear Lord, help us find ways to restore our love for each other. When the family is broken, our lives are disrupted. We need to hear from you, oh Lord. If we don't hear from you, the family union will suffer greatly. There is no problem that you cannot solve. Please help us renew our marriage vows, and help cheating spouses stop making decision that will destroy our families.

Thank you, dear Lord, for ministering to cheating spouses. Amen.

Scripture reading: Gen. 3:16, Isa. 54:5, Mark 10:12, 1 Cor. 7:14, 2 Cor. 11:2, Eph. 5:23–25, Exod. 25:17, Prov. 18:22, Eccles.9:9, Luke 17:32, Eph. 5:28

CHAPTER 45

Prayer for Good Books to Read

eavenly Father, you have given us the Bible as a landmark to guide our daily lives. In this book, we find redemption, peace, joy, and love. From Genesis to Revelation, you have provided guidelines for us to follow. If we obey your word, we will have eternal life. Our society has shifted from the living word, and for this reason we are faced with chaos in our world. Help your people read the Bible daily so that they will have a well-balanced life. We pray that authors of other books will write meaningfully to bring glory and honor to your name. King David wrote many psalms and hymns that bring solace to our souls. He wrote in Psalm 23:1, "The Lord is my shepherd, I shall not want" for when we are afraid. He also wrote in Psalm 100:1, "Make a joyful noise unto the Lord all ye lands" for when we are sad. Let us always be mindful that reading the Bible will inspire us to gain wisdom and knowledge about your word.

Thank you, dear Lord, for providing us with knowledge. Amen.

Scripture reading: Gen. 1:50, Ps. 23:1, Ps.100:1

CHAPTER 46

Prayer for Good Shows to Watch on Television

Dear Lord, we are living in a world in which television is a part of our daily lives. Some children spend most of their time watching television. Lord, please guide the leaders of our nation to set better standards for what is being showed on television. Our minds sometime go astray because of constant violence that is being showed in a repetitious manner. We need your guidance in our lives so that we can make better choices about what we watch on television. Help us to be more selective with the kind of programs that we allow our children to watch. Our children are sometimes faced with added stress and disruption because of what they watch on television. Please inspire godly producers who will take the time to write inspiring stories that will help our children learn good habits instead of stealing, killing, and being unkind to each other. You alone can change the hearts of mankind. Many good things can be learned from the medium of television if you grant wisdom to those who are suitable to produce good programs.

Thank you, dear Lord, for providing good shows for us to watch. Amen.

Scripture reading: 1 Peter 4:7–19, Ps. 141:3–4, Mark 13:33–37

CHAPTER 47

Prayer for Pens, Paper, and Pencils to Write

Heavenly Father, you are the same yesterday, and you will be the same tomorrow; you change not. In Exodus 34:1, you said to Moses, "Hew thee two tables of stone like unto the first, and I will write upon these tables the words that were in the first tables, which thou breakest.". Just as you supplied Moses with writing equipment, I pray for our children here in America and around the world that they will get writing paper, pencils, pens, and all their school supplies so that they can write what you would have them write. Many children are lacking the basic supplies needed to enrich their lives. All things are possible when we believe. Please touch the hearts and minds of your people to help those who are in need of these supplies. When we equip our children with the tools needed to excel in writing skills, our society will be more productive.

Thank you, dear Lord, for hearing and answering our feeble prayer in Jesus's name. Amen.

Scripture reading: Exod. 34:1

CHAPTER 48

Prayer for Wisdom

Most heavenly Father, thank you for all things both new and old. You have given so much to your people here on earth, even when we don't deserve your goodness. We are asking you to bless us with wisdom so that we can plan for our future. Without wisdom from above, we will make mistakes in our lives that will cause us pain and suffering. 1 Kings 4:3 states "And Solomon's wisdom excelled the wisdom of all the children of the east country, and all the wisdom of Egypt." Because you are the giver of all good gifts, King Solomon was able to be successful in all he did. We are thankful, Lord, for the example given in Solomon's life. If you granted it for King Solomon, I am sure you will do the same for all who ask you for wisdom. Please help all your children around the world to read your word and meditate day and night. Wisdom will lead us into understanding your word. Help us keep our hearts pure so that your wisdom will always flow through us.

Thank you, dear Lord, for granting us wisdom. Amen.

Scripture reading: 1 Kings 4:29–34, Job 28:28, Ps. 111:10, Prov. 4:5, Prov. 16:16, Matt. 11:19

CHAPTER 49

Prayer for a Discerning Spirit

Lord, I pray that you will help us examine ourselves and realize that you are coming soon. We need to have a discerning spirit so that we can live a holy life in this troubled world. King Solomon was able to discern the mother of the child. 1 Kings 3:27 states, "Then the king answered and said, give her the living child and in no wise slay it: she is the mother thereof.". You gave a discerning spirit to King Solomon so that he could make the right decision when two women were in crisis. Help your people study your word so that we can learn more of you. Unless you give a discerning heart to your children, we will not be able to focus on your word.

Thank you, dear Lord, for the gift of a discerning spirit. Amen.

Scripture reading: 1 Kings 3:24–28, Eccl. 8:5, 1 Cor. 11:29, Heb. 5:14

CHAPTER 50

Prayer to Witness the Living Word of God

D ear Lord, in John 8:12 you said, "I am the light of the world.". Please give us the ability to witness your word to others. You taught your disciples that they must "go out into the highways and hedges and compel them to come in." I pray that we here on earth will tell others about your marvelous word. Your word is truth and life. We must share the good news so that others will come to know you. As we journey in this land, let us be mindful of the price you paid on Calvary for our sins. Fill us with the gift of the Holy Spirit that miracles will follow in our lives as we share your word with others. So many people need to know about the true vine; your word is truth, oh, Lord. Thank you, Lord, for giving each of us a mind to follow in your footsteps as we win souls for your kingdom. Touch the hearts of men and women as we witness your word in Jesus's name.

Thank you, dear Lord, for the living word of God. Amen.

Scripture readings: Gen. 31:48, Job 10:19, Job 11:10, Ps. 89:37, Isa. 43:10, Mal. 2:14, Matt. 24:14, Luke 14:23, John 8:12, John 8:59, Rev. 1:5

CHAPTER 51

Prayer to Obey God's Word

Precious Lord, from the dawn of creation, you have provided guidelines for your children to follow. Help us to be obedient to your will and your ways. 1 Samuel 15:22 states, "And Samuel said, 'Hath the LORD as great delight in burnt offerings and sacrifices, as in obeying the voice of the LORD? Behold, to obey is better than sacrifice, and to hearken than the fat of rams.'" So many times we fail in our plans because we refuse to obey your word. When Israel obeyed your word, its people enjoyed victory. When they were rebellious and disobedient, they suffered defeat. Lord, help us seek guidance daily by reading and meditating on your written word. If we are obedient, we will gain victory and make it into heaven.

Thank you, dear Lord, for helping us obey God's word. Amen.

Scripture reading: Exod. 33:1–23, 1 Sam. 15:22, Acts 5:29, Eph. 6:1, Col. 3:22, Heb. 13:17

CHAPTER 52

Prayer to Be Filled with the Holy Spirit

Sweet Jesus, you told your disciples that when you returned to heaven, you would send the Holy Spirit to all who would receive it. We thank you, Lord, for the gift of the Holy Spirit. Without the Holy Spirit, we would not be able to witness to unbelievers. Without the Holy Spirit, it would be impossible to live free from sin. To be filled with the Holy Spirit is a gift that only you can give. We thank you, Lord, for paying the price with your life on Calvary. If you anoint us with the Holy Spirit, we will be ready to do your will. Paul wrote in Ephesians 5:18–19, "And be not drunk with wine, wherein is excess; but be filled with the Spirit, speaking to yourselves in psalms and hymns and spiritual songs, singing and making melody in your heart to the Lord."

Thank you, dear Lord, for pouring out the Holy Spirit upon us so that we can make peace with those who sometimes mistreat us without cause. Amen.

Scripture reading: Acts 2:1–47

CHAPTER 53

Prayer for Evildoers to Change and Seek God

ost Gracious God, you are the giver of life. When you created the world, all things were pleasant in your sight. After the fall of man, sin came into the world. We pray, dear Lord, that those who commit evil will turn from their evil ways and seek your face once more. No evildoer can enter into your holy sanctuary. When Saul was on his way to Damascus to persecute the saints, he was changed when "suddenly there shone from heaven a great light round about him." His name was changed from Saul to Paul. Saul did much evil to the saints in Jerusalem. Lord, you had mercy on him, and his life was changed because of your goodness and loving-kindness. You told Ananias in Acts 9:15 that "He was a chosen vessel unto you, to bear your name before the Gentiles, and kings, and the children of Israel.". Even though we have committed evil, you still show us love and mercy. Help us, dear Lord, to be more like Paul and less like Saul. Teach us to read your word, repent from our sins, and sow seeds of kindness to each other. In Psalm 34:14, you declare that we should "depart from evil, and do good; seek peace, and pursue it." It is only by reading and studying your word that we can refrain from doing evil in this world.

Thank you, dear Lord, for changing evildoers. Amen.

Scripture reading: Ps. 34:14, Prov. 3:7, Prov. 5:3, Matt. 5:11, Matt. 6:34, Matt. 7:11, Acts 9: 13, Acts 22:6, Rom. 7:19, Rom. 12:21, 1 Tim. 6:10, 1 Thess. 5:22

CHAPTER 54

Prayer for Our Enemies

Dear Lord, we are living in an unfriendly world. Many people hate each other for reasons unknown to us. You are the bread of life. Solomon wrote in Proverbs 25:21–22, "If thine enemy be hungry, give him bread to eat; if he be thirsty, give him water to drink; for thou shalt heap coals of fire upon his head, and the Lord shall reward thee." Sometimes we find it hard to love our enemies, but you have showed us the way by going to the cross. We must forgive others to make it into your kingdom. Teach us, dear Lord, to pray in earnest each day for our enemies. If we pray for them, you will reward us with your loving-kindness and your tender mercies. You have instructed us in your word how to live a good Christian life, and you will help us when we are weak, when we can't see our way, and when we can't see how we are to forgive our enemies. Please point us to Calvary, and this will surely change our lives. Because you have forgiven us of our sins, then we ought to forgive our enemies.

We pray, dear Lord, that you will answer this prayer in your loving name. Amen.

Scripture reading: Ps. 23:5, Prov. 25:21, Matt. 5:44, Rom. 5:10, James 4:4

CHAPTER 55

Prayer for Lack of Provision

Dear Lord, so many people are living below their standard because of lack of provision for themselves and their families. Help those who have much to be mindful of those who are in need. I pray that you will open doors that are closed so that people can find jobs to support themselves. David wrote in Psalm 23:1, "The Lord is my Shepherd, I shall not want." Nothing is impossible with you, dear Lord. If we ask by faith and believe, you will guide the way. Mark 10:21 states, "Then Jesus beholding him loved him, and said unto him, One thing thou lackest: go thy way, sell whatsoever thou hast, and give to the poor, and thou shall have treasure in heaven: and come, take up the cross, and follow me." Teach us, Lord, how to follow in your footsteps. When we seek you first, we will never be in need of anything. You alone can give good gifts. All things come from you.

Thank you, Heavenly Father, for keeping us from lacking what we need. Amen.

Scripture reading: Gen. 42:25–28, Ps. 23:1, Mark 10:21–30, Acts 4:34

CHAPTER 56

Prayer for Parents and Families Who Have Lost Loved Ones

Most heavenly Father, we come before you once more asking you to grant peace and abiding love to all parents and families around the word who have lost loved ones. When death comes to a child, it is frightening for parents. You are the giver of life. Please help all those who are hurting today because the sting of death has visited their homes. Let us be mindful that when the sting of death has crushed our frail bodies here on Earth, we will be joined with you and the angels in heaven, where death will never conquer our bodies anymore. While Jesus was on earth, many people who were lame and at the point of death were made whole. We thank you, Lord, for all your goodness and mercies that you have given to us.

Help us dear Lord, find comfort in reading your word, which has been provided to guide our daily lives as we journey here on earth.

Thank you, dear Lord, for hearing and answering this prayer. Amen.

Scripture reading: John 4:6–54

CHAPTER 57

Prayer for Those Who Are Suffering with Pain

Dear Lord, pain can cause one to lose his or her senses at any given moment. Please look down from your dwelling place and heal all those who are suffering with pain in their minds and bodies. We were made from the dust of the earth, and you breathed the breath of life into us. You know our bodies, and you know when we are in pain. Sometimes, dear Lord, we cannot express the suffering we feel because of pain. Please lighten our heavy burdens because of pain. When Jesus went to the cross, he took our infirmities with him. Jesus bore the pain for our sins so that we can be free of pain and suffering. Remind us, Lord, that you and you alone can give us deliverance when we are burdened with pain. We humbly ask for your healing power in our lives this day in Jesus's precious name. Amen.

Thank you, dear Lord, for hearing and answering this prayer. Amen.

Scripture reading: Matt. 7:7

CHAPTER 58

Prayer for Good Vision to See and Read God's Word

Oh, Lord, our God, you are mighty in heaven and on earth. We come once more to ask for your blessings upon our eyes. Good vision is necessary for your children to read and study your word.. In John 9:1–25, you restored sight to the man who was born blind. This was truly a miracle from above. When we have good vision, we are able to see all of your creations here on earth. When we look at the sky above with good vision, we can see the stars that you have placed in the skies. Help us, Lord, to seek your blessing always for good vision as long as we live.

Thank you, dear Lord, for good vision. Amen.

Scripture reading: Matt. 9:1–40, John 9:1–25

CHAPTER 59

Prayer to Give God the First Fruits

The Earth is the Lord's and the fullness thereof. All things belong to Him in heaven and on earth. Help us, dear Lord, to give of ourselves to you. Our finances are yours; our lives are yours. You have created all our possessions. We pray, dear Lord, that we will give the first fruits to you so that blessings will continue to flow into our lives and to all our generations. Malachi 3:10 reads, "Bring ye all the tithes into the storehouse, that there may be meat in mine house, and prove me now herewith, saith the LORD of hosts, if I will not open you the windows of heaven, and pour you out a blessing, that there shall not be room enough to receive it.". Please give us wisdom to study your word and seek more of your grace so that as we give to you, we will never be in need of anything.

Thank you, dear Lord, for hearing this prayer. Amen.

Scripture reading: Ezek. 44:30, Mal. 3:10

CHAPTER 60

Prayer for Good Health

Precious Lord, because of our sins, our bodies are weak and frail. We humbly ask you to restore good health to us. You went to the cross so that we could have redemption from sin. Help us seek more of you by praying and reading your word daily. Good health is a part of your plan for all believers. Lord, you declare that above all things, you want us to be prosperous and to be in good health. Thank you, Lord, for all that you have done for us. Please keep us safe each day from all harm and danger as we pass through this world. Satan tries to cast pain and suffering on your children, but we know that you can heal sickness and disease when we pray and believe. .

Thank you, dear Lord, for the gift of good health. Amen.

Scripture reading: 2 Kings 20:1–21

CHAPTER 61

Prayer for Caregivers

Dear Lord, we are thankful for all the special people you have placed in this world who are kind and true to others—those who care for the sick, the lame, and the poor. We ask for special blessings upon them. Caregivers are sometimes the unsung heroes. We are thankful for the love and wisdom you have placed in these wonderful human beings. Thank you, Lord, for sending good caregivers who give more than enough and who don't ask for much in return. Lord, I am reminded of the woman who baked the cake for Elijah. Such compassion could come only from you, dear Lord. Help us to be good caregivers to those who are in need.

Thank you, Lord, for those who give care. Amen.

Scripture reading: 2 Kings 17:1–24

CHAPTER 62

Prayer for Hospitals around the World

Most excellent Father, you are the healer of the universe. We are living in a world in which people need a secure place to get well when they are sick. I pray for hospitals around the world this day. We need hospitals that are equipped with modern technology to save the lives of our loved ones. Many hospitals cannot function because of a lack of funds and personnel. Please open the hearts of your people to give to hospitals around the world so that lives can be saved. When you were on earth, you healed the sick and the lame. Today, we pray for healing in Jesus's name upon all those who are hurting in mind and body. Send your blessing down upon all hospitals so that they will open their doors to the poor and needy around the world.

Thank you, dear Lord, for providing hospitals. Amen.

Scripture reading: Matt. 8:17, James 5:14–15, 1 Pet. 4:9

CHAPTER 63

Prayer for Law Enforcement Officers

Heavenly Father, you are the enforcer of all laws. Grace and truth come from you. I pray that you will guide all those who work in law enforcement. We need laws in our lives so that we will be able to live and work without discrimination. From the foundation of the world, God set standards for man to follow. Moses received laws from you and passed them on to govern mankind. We thank you, Lord, for all of your commandments. Help us, dear Lord, to be mindful of laws that are set for us today. If we obey the law, then we will have a happier life in this world. Please help all law enforcement officers to be just and kind to each other. We pray that you will guide each and every one of us to live within the laws so that we can have peace within our hearts and minds.

Thank you, dear Lord, for law enforcement officers. Amen.

Scripture reading: Gen. 49:10, Isa. 33:22, John 1:17

CHAPTER 64

Prayer for Transportation

ost gracious Lord, we thank you for making it possible for us to have reliable transportation each day. In our daily lives, we must work. Without buses, cars, and trains, it would be difficult to move from place to place each day. So Lord, please keep us safe as we travel along the highways and the byways. Help us to be mindful of each other's safety. Sometimes we forget to share our cars with those who cannot afford one. Teach us to show mercy and love to each other. Without reliable transportation, we would have a much harder life—perhaps more difficult than we could bear.

We thank you, dear Lord, for providing transportation for us. Amen.

CHAPTER 65

Prayer for People Who Are Living Alternative Lifestyles

Dear Lord, you are the great "I am that I am." You have created both males and females for a special purpose here on earth. We pray that you will speak to the hearts of all those who have strayed away from the teaching you have given in your word. Many people choose to live lifestyles that do not meet the guidelines of your word. You are the only one who can change lives and make them brand new. Please meet the needs of all your children who have chosen to live alternative lifestyles. Help them seek guidance in your word and find comfort and peace as they journey here on earth. Your word declares that *no* sin can enter into heaven. We must repent and turn away from all sin. Please forgive them of all their sins and transgressions.

Thank you, dear Lord, for hearing and answering this prayer. Amen.

Scripture reading: Matt. 3:2, Matt. 9:13, Luke 13:3–5, 1 John 3:9

CHAPTER 66

Prayer for Our Pilots and Crew Workers

D ear Lord, our airline pilots and crew work very hard to keep us safe as they fly the airplanes. We are so grateful that you have given them the ability to fly and maintain the aircrafts with such skill. Please protect all pilots and workers as they do their best to make us safe as we travel around the world. Many times we forget to say thank you after a successful landing. Help us be mindful that you have given wisdom to those who seek to do well. Please continue to guide our pilots and crew daily.

Thank you, dear Lord, for hearing and answering this prayer. Amen.

Scripture Reading: Matthew 4:18-22

CHAPTER 67

Prayer for Our Fishermen Who Travel on the Deep Sea

ord, you have created the heaven and the earth. You have called the seas into existence. Today, the sea is a way of life to obtain food for your children here on earth. Many men and women risk their lives on a daily basis to catch fish. We pray for guidance as they travel on the seas. Please protect them from harm and danger, both seen and unseen. Please help them take just enough from the sea that the next generation will be able to survive as we have done.

Thank you, Lord, for protecting those who travel the seas. Amen.

CHAPTER 68

Prayer to Be Anointed with the Holy Spirit

Lord, just as you anointed your son, David, with the oil of gladness, we pray that you will anoint your sons and daughters one more time. We need the anointing of the Holy Spirit to guide us to make the right decisions in our lives. We are living in a world that is full of confusion and distrust. Please send down a fresh anointing upon your people this day. Sorrow has taken over our land instead of joy. No more can we sit idly in this land. Come, Holy Spirit, and refresh our hearts today. Surely you can see in the heart of man that we have lost our first love. Samuel anointed David just as you have commanded according to your word in 1 Samuel 16:13. He was a blessing in the land. Today we need the same kind of blessing in our hearts. When the Holy Spirit is in control of our hearts, we will learn to love our fellow men.

Thank you for hearing this prayer in Jesus's name. Amen.

Scripture reading: 1 Sam. 16:13

CHAPTER 69

Prayer for the Restoration of God's House

Loving Father and creator of the universe, we pray that you will restore your temple so that your children will be able to worship once more in peace and love. Please send workers to build churches around the world so that all can hear the good news of salvation. Men and women, boys and girls need to return to the living word. Surely, Lord, you can restore your house of worship so that our hearts will be renewed with your word. We are burdened with problems on various levels, and only your word can give us victory to sustain our lives in this world. Through your grace and mercy, we will win the victory.

Thank you, dear Lord, for hearing and answering this prayer. Amen.

Scripture reading: Ezra 6:1–22 (Focus on verse 5.)

CHAPTER 70

Prayer for Our Sanitation Workers

recious Lord, please keep our sanitation workers free from all danger. Prevent those who pick up our garbage and dispose of it from getting sick because of their exposure to waste.. These are men and women who leave their homes from day to day to keep our environment safe. We thank you, Lord, for protecting them as they do their task each day. Sanitation workers are sometimes forgotten at Christmas time when gifts are given out to friends and loved ones. Help us pray each day for them. Lord, you have the power to bless all people. We ask for a special blessing upon all sanitation workers all around the world.

Thank you, dear Lord, for sanitation workers. Amen.

Scripture reading: Ps. 8:3–9, 2 Thess. 3:10

CHAPTER 71

Prayer for All Those Who Garden

Dear Lord, you created the first garden in Eden, and you placed Adam in charge to care for it. We pray that you will send a special blessing to all those who take time out to plant a garden. Planting seeds of flowers and fruits enriches our lives each and every day. Please bless all gardeners around the world. We thank you, Lord, for the butterflies that visit the gardens and for the bees that pollinate the crops. Certainly you have given all that we need here on earth. When the flowers are in bloom and the beautiful aroma fills the air, we remember that you made it possible.

Thank you, dear Lord, for your blessing on our gardeners. Amen.

Scripture reading: Gen. 1:26–31, Gen. 2:1–18

CHAPTER 72

Prayer for Those Who Stock the Shelves in Our Grocery Stores

ord, you have said that "if any would not work, neither should he eat." We pray for all those who stock the shelves in our grocery stores. This is a tedious job for many, but they work to make a living each day. Please help us to say thank you when we come into contact with the store clerks. Everyone has a job to do; may they do it well, knowing that they, too, are giving back to our society each day.

Thank you, dear Lord, for hearing and answering this prayer. Amen.

Scripture reading: 2Thess. 3:10

CHAPTER 73

Prayer for Those Who Build Our Sewer System

Heavenly Father, so many people are living in this world in a safer environment because of those who build and treat our sewer lines. Our health is not compromised because of being exposed to waste material. We thank you, Lord, for giving these men and women the knowledge to treat our sewers so that contamination will not enter into our water system. Please guide them as they work each and every day to make this world a safer place to live in. Surely their reward is in heaven for all the good they have done for your children here on earth. Help us, dear Lord, pray for their safety as they care for our sewer system. We humbly ask your blessings for all sewer workers around the world.

Thank you, dear Lord, for those who build sewers. Amen.

CHAPTER 74

Prayer for Our Firefighters

Oh, Lord, our God, how excellent is your name in all the earth. We pray for all our firefighters around the world who risk their lives on a daily basis to save others. Please help us prevent fires by making sure all of our electrical equipment is maintained. Firefighters have to be ready, rain or shine, to perform their duties without delay. Thank you, Lord, for guiding all firefighters for the special work they do. Fighting fires is a difficult job, dear Lord, so please keep them in the palm of your hand from day to day.

Thank you, dear Lord, for hearing and answering this prayer. Amen.

CHAPTER 75

Prayer for Those Who Protect Our Missiles

Dear Lord, our world is full of hate and mistrust among nations. We must protect ourselves from our enemies. We pray for all those who protect our missiles. Help them secure all missiles from the wrong hands. We pray that peace will return in the world once more, for then we will not have any need for missiles that can take lives away. Remind us that we were made to serve you and not to hurt each other.

Thank you for hearing and answering this prayer. Amen.

CHAPTER 76

Prayer for Our President

Most gracious Lord, we thank you for the leader of our land. The president is faced with many decisions that must be made on a daily basis. Please give him wisdom greater than before. You have the power to make all things right. Our president needs daily guidance that only you can give. Protect him with your heavenly blessings. The president cannot function unless he hears from you and learns to trust you. Dear Lord, please open his mind to wisdom so that he will come to depend on you and you alone.

Thank you, dear Lord, for hearing and answering this prayer. Amen.

CHAPTER 77

Prayer for Our Federal Agents

Dear Lord, we pray that you will give all of our federal agents wisdom as they protect our land. Our agents are faced with many critical decisions each day. Help them seek guidance from your word before they take a case. Please help all citizens to live a godly life so that we can all live in a world that is free from hurt and danger. When you created the universe, all things were pleasing in your sight. Renew our hearts daily so that we will do more of what is right and less of what is wrong. Please keep all of our agents free from unseen dangers around the world and at home.

Thank you, dear Lord, for hearing and answering this prayer. Amen.

CHAPTER 78

Prayer for Our National Guard

ear Heavenly Father, creator of the universe, we come to you once more and ask your blessings upon our National Guard. Without your protection and wisdom, our National Guard will not be able to carry out its duties from day to day. Please shine your heavenly blessings on these men and women as they travel near and far throughout the land. Sometimes, our National Guard is called to do tasks that are seemingly impossible. Lord, please keep them safe from unseen dangers. Remember them just as you have watched over your children in times past. Many of our National Guardsmen and women are faced with decisions to be made in a split second to save lives. Those are the times when they need you most. You have power and love for all your children.

Thank you, dear Lord, for watching over our National Guard and keeping its men and women safe each and every day. Amen.

Scripture reading: Gen. 31:49, Matt. 24:42–46, Matt. 26:41, 1 Pet. 4:7

CHAPTER 79

Prayer for Our Ministers and All Clergy

Dear Lord, we come in your name to ask mercy and blessing upon all your ministering servants. You have given the great commission years ago that we must win the lost and dying for your cause. When you went to the cross, you took all our infirmities and our sorrows so that we can spread the good news of redemption. Each and every one of us is called to tell others about your name. If we are willing to spread the good news, salvation will be for us and all those who believe. There are different ways for us to minister. Healing and deliverance come from you. Peter told the lame man in Acts 3 that he did not have silver or gold to give, but he gave him your name, and the man was made whole. Bless all ministers around the world who will keep their minds and focus on your return. Many ministers are turning away from the faith each day. However, you promised in Revelation 2:10, "Be thou faithful unto death, and I will give you a crown of life.". Life is for all believers, so please help our ministers and all clergy study your word on a daily basis and seek guidance. Help them to be prayerful and watchful because Satan is always looking and trying to destroy your chosen vessels.

We thank you, dear Lord, for hearing and answering this prayer in Jesus's name. Amen.

Scripture reading: Ps. 103:21, Matt. 20:26, Acts 3:6, 2 Tim. 4:5, Rev. 2:10

CHAPTER 80

Prayer for Peace in the Middle East

Oh, Lord, our God, how excellent is your name in all the earth. Father, you have given this land to your children for an inheritance because of Abraham's love for you. Today, the Middle East is divided into many territories because of religious beliefs. We pray for peace in the Middle East. We pray that they will revisit Mount Olive, where you prayed with your disciples, while you were living here on earth. In John 14:27, you said, "Peace I leave with you, my peace I give unto you: not as the world giveth, give I unto you. Let not your heart be troubled, neither let it be afraid.". Fear has caused mistrust in the Middle East. Men and women in that region need to hear from you once more. The word of God is the only remedy for fear and mistrust. Lord, please raise up men and women with a vision of peace instead of war and hate. We are living in the last days, and we can see the fulfillment of your words upon the Middle East. The answer lies in prayer.

Lord, please send a revival to the land as on the day of Pentecost, when every nation will understand each other through tongues.

Unless you revive your people, we all will be lost. Help us fast, pray, and seek repentance before it is too late. You went to Calvary for all people, dear Lord. Redemption must start at the cross.

Thank you, dear Lord, for hearing and answering this prayer in Jesus's name. Amen.

Scripture reading: John 14:27, John 16:33, Acts 2, Rom. 5:1, Rom. 10:15, Phil. 4:7, Col. 3:15, Heb. 12:14

CHAPTER 81

Prayer for the Whole World

F ather, you are worthy to be praised "from the rising of the sun unto the going down of the same." In you there is life, peace, love, and contentment. Thank you for this day that you have made. Thank you for this world that you have made. Out of nothing, you formed this majestic universe called earth. No one told you what animal to create; you just knew what to do. We humbly ask you to bless the whole world. The land is vastly slipping away into perversion, and mankind doesn't know what to do anymore. The answer lies in your word. You said in 2 Chronicles 7:14, "If my people, which are called by my name, shall humble themselves, and pray, and seek my face, and turn from their wicked ways; then will I hear from heaven, and will forgive their sin, and will heal their land."

The world needs healing that can come only from you. Yesterday's blessing will not work for us today. We need a fresh anointing each and every day. When you made the world, it was pleasing in your sight until man corrupted the land. Please help each and every one of us to turn from our sins and seek your grace. Many people are traveling over the world seeking peace but cannot find it. Mankind has taken to the skies in search of more knowledge but lacks the ability to love one another in passing each day when walking the streets. We need a double portion of your spirit in our hearts so that we can see what is truly right for our lives. Help us read your holy word daily and help those who are truly in need. Then and only then will our world yield peace so that mankind will feel some fulfillment as we wait for your return.

Thank you, dear Lord, for hearing this prayer in Jesus's name. Amen.

Scripture reading: Prov. 15:8, Matt. 21:13, Matt. 21:22, Acts 6:4, James 5:15–16, Rev. 5:8.

CHAPTER 82

Prayer for Mothers Who Are in Travail to Give Birth

Dear Heavenly Father, you have created woman for a special task—to bear children. Thank you for blessing our wombs. When you created woman, you did not intend for her to bear such a heavy burden, but because of sin, each woman pays a heavy price to bring a child into the world. After Eve sinned in the Garden of Eden, her punishment was extended. You said in Genesis 3:16, "Unto the woman I will greatly multiply thy sorrow and thy conceptions: In sorrow thou shalt bring forth children; and thy desire shall be to thy husband and he shall rule over thee." From that day, women all around the world have paid a high price to bring children into this world. We pray and ask forgiveness for our sins. Please remember those women who have travailed to bring forth life into this world. Giving birth is truly a miracle from the throne of God. In spite of our sins, you have showed love and compassion for us. Thank you for mercy and grace for everyone who has given birth to a child. Help mothers around the world to be kind and loving to their children and all other children each and every day. You are the giver of life.

We thank you for such a special gift in Jesus' Name. Amen.

Scripture reading: Gen. 3:16

CHAPTER 83

Prayer for Single Parents

Most Heavenly Father, you have given so much to us even when we don't deserve your kindness. We pray for single parents all over the world. Parents become single for various reasons. Sometimes divorce causes one parent to leave the home. Sometimes death steals one parent away. Sometimes, because of sin, one parent might be placed in jail. Whatever the situation, sometimes parents find themselves raising their children alone. You are a merciful father in spite of our situations. Grant peace and love to all single parents. Guide all single parents with wisdom and understanding. Help them read your word over their children and speak life for prosperity as long as they live. We are mindful that you can do all things when we seek guidance from you. Please provide shelter and food for all single parents so that their households will be full.

Thank you, dear Lord, for hearing and answering this prayer in Jesus's name. Amen.

Scripture reading: John 9:1–4, Eph. 6:1

CHAPTER 84

Prayer for Broken Homes

Dear Lord, you went to the cross to redeem your children from all sins and sorrows. You took our sins upon your body so that we might be free. Please look down upon all those who have found themselves living in broken homes. So many homes are broken because of betrayal from spouses who have neglected their family duties. Whatever may be the cause, you are the only one who can bring joy and peace to these broken homes. Many lives will never be the same without your grace and mercy. Help those who are hurting because they live in a broken home to find refuge in your word each and every day. Please remember the children who sometimes suffer because one parent moves out of these homes. There are homes that are broken because a spouse went home to be with you in heaven. Please help such families connect or reconnect to you because you are the reason for our being. Help all people around the world to pray for one another so that peace and love will flow throughout the universe in all broken homes.

Thank you, dear Lord, for hearing and answering this prayer. Amen.

Scripture reading: Ps. 51:17, Prov. 19:14, Mark 3:25, John 14:2, John 19:36, Acts 2:46, Eph. 2:14, 1 Tim. 5:8

CHAPTER 85

Prayer for Broken Dreams

Precious Lord, over the years, so many people's dreams have been broken because their dreams were not right for them. Many times, parents have a dream for their children, only to find that it was their dream and not their child's. Whatever it is, this is a broken dream. . Please, Lord, help such people seek your guidance before their hearts and minds are broken. Some dreams are not in your will for many of your children. For this reason, those dreams do not materialize. You are the only one who prevents one from having broken dreams. In 1 Peter 5:7, your word says "Casting all your care upon him, for he careth for you." We need to know what your good and perfect will is for our lives so that when we dream, it will be what you truly have in mind for us. May all your children find comfort in reading and searching your word more and more each day so that we will find meaning in our lives instead of having broken dreams that are not in your plans.

Thank you, dear Lord, for leading and guiding us into your perfect will. Amen.

Scripture reading: Matt. 13:22, Luke 21:34, 1 Pet. 5:7

CHAPTER 86

Prayer for Daily Guidance

Dear Lord, many years ago, you spoke with Moses and told him you needed him to talk to your people. He could not have done your work without your guidance. We thank you, Lord, for guiding your children throughout the ages. Today, we pray that you will show us favor as we journey through this land. When we seek your help, you will never leave us alone. In Psalm 46:1, King David said, you are a "present help in time of trouble." And in Psalm 46:7, King David said, "The Lord of host is with us, the God of Jacob is our refuge." When we place our lives into your hands, then we don't have to worry where we are going because you will lead us in the right direction. Only a loving father who cares for his children will be able to guide us as long as we shall live. So, dear Lord, as we travel from place to place, please guide our footsteps in the right direction. Help us be kind to those we meet along our journey. Help us to tell the glorious story of how you brought salvation down to man by giving your life on Calvary.

Lord, keep us in your perfect will as we travel each and every day. Amen.

Scripture reading: Luke 1:79, John 16:13

CHAPTER 87

Prayer for Decision Making

Dear Lord, when you decided to make this world, you made it out of nothing. You spoke it into existence. However, for mankind to make decisions, we must focus on your will. Please grant us wisdom when making decisions. Making the right decision will enable your children to enjoy peace and love throughout our lives. Sometimes, the decisions that we make can cause us to lose control of our entire lives. People often pick up bad habits that will lead them into unseen danger. Without your presence in our lives, we will fail in whatever we do. King David said, "My heart is inditing a good matter." When we focus on your word and pray, we will be able to make good decisions. We cannot fail when we trust you each and every day. Making a good decision paid off when Jesus went to the cross. If He had refused the cross, then the world would still be in darkness after Adam's sin.

Thank you, dear Lord, for making it possible for us to come to you with a broken heart. Help us make good decisions for our lives. Amen.

Scripture reading: Ps. 45:1

CHAPTER 88

Prayer to Hold Our Peace when Faced with Trouble

D ear Lord, we are living in a world that is full of constant violence. People are not safe in their homes or on their jobs. Even in the sanctuary, crime has taken hold. Please help us hold our peace when we are faced with trouble. Help us pray and seek courage from you. You were wounded for our transgressions, and you were faithful even to the cross. Send your holy angels to guide us when we are burdened by the cares of this world. When you were on earth, you spoke peace to everyone who would listen. Our nation is faced with all kinds of problems today, but if we hold our peace and seek your guidance, we will be victorious in the end. Trouble is all around our cities, but with you on our side, we will win the victory. Help us pray for each other each and every day.

Thank you, dear Lord, for all the love you have given us. Please keep our nation in the palm of your hands. Please let your word speak peace instead of war.

May your grace rest upon us always. Amen.

Scripture reading: Eccl. 3:8, Prov. 11:12, Isa. 48:18, Luke 2:14, John 14:27, Rom. 5:1, 1 Thess. 5:21, 1 Tim. 1:19, Titus 1:9, Heb. 4:14, Rev. 2:13

CHAPTER 89
Prayer to Speak Truth Always

Most gracious Lord, you have given instruction in your word that your "word is truth," according to John 17:17. Help us speak truth always so that we can live a life free from sin. When our conscience is free, we are able to relax and enjoy the beautiful creations you have given us. In Psalm 91:4, King David said, "His truth shall be thy shield and buckler." Truth is our passport to make it in our society. If we don't tell the truth, we can cause much harm to ourselves and those who we come in contact with. We must speak the truth always because it is the right thing to do. Jesus is truth, and we must live as Christ did in order to make it into God's kingdom. Forgive us of our sins, dear Lord, and help us to be truthful always.

Thank you, dear Lord, for hearing and answering our prayer. Amen.

Scripture reading: Ps. 51:6, Ps. 91:4, John 8:32, John 14:16, John 17:17

CHAPTER 90

Prayer Not to Steal

reat heavenly Father, you have given your precious word to guide us in our daily walk with you each and every day. You gave Moses, your servant, special guidelines for us to follow here on earth. In Exodus 20:15, it is written, "Thou shalt not steal.". You gave instructions to Moses that have been passed down from generation to generation. If we obey your laws, we will be free from evil and condemnation. Many people steal from their neighbors, and sometimes lives are lost when people steal what is not theirs. Help us, heavenly Father, refrain from stealing and follow the guidelines you have given for us to be content here on earth. So much sorrow and pain come to people because of the loss of their possessions. Please speak to the hearts of those who would steal from the innocent. Help such persons to return all stolen property and give their lives totally over to your will. Your word declares in Revelation 19:11, "Ye shall not steal neither deal falsely." We pray this day that all those who have stolen will steal no more but repent of their sins and turn their lives completely over to your will and your ways.

Thank you, precious Lord, for hearing and answering this prayer. Amen.

Scripture reading: Exod. 20:15, Lev. 19:1

CHAPTER 91
Prayer Not to Tell a Lie

Dear Lord, we come before you asking you to guide our hearts and minds into doing what is right. Help us tell the truth always and refrain from telling lies. In Exodus 20:16, your word declares that, "Thou shall not bear false witness against thy neighbor." Lying will cause man to be separated from having fellowship with you. Help us, dear Lord, to pray, read your word, and declare righteousness over the land instead of speaking lies. Many homes are suffering because of lies that are told from day to day. Satan lied to the woman in the Garden of Eden, and today people continue to lie to each other. We need to hear from you each day so that we can do what is right. We all will perish unless we return and seek to do your will. In Psalm 37:11, King David said, "The meek shall inherit the earth and shall delight themselves in the abundance of peace." No liars will inherit the kingdom of God. Only those who are pure and blood-washed will enter into your rest. We are confident that you will keep us in your perfect will, sustain us with everlasting wisdom, and keep us from telling lies.

Thank you, dear Lord, for hearing and answering this prayer. Amen.

Scripture reading: Exod. 20:16, Gen. 3:4, Ps. 119:104, Prov. 6:19

CHAPTER 92

Prayer Not to Be Covetous

Father, you have given everyone the ability to prosper in this world. If we work and give back a portion of what we have to continue your work here on earth, blessings will follow us as long as we shall live. In Exodus 20:17 your word says, "Thou shalt not covet thy neighbor's house, thou shalt not covet thy neighbor's wife, nor his man servant, nor his maid servant, nor his ass, nor anything that is thy neighbor's." Lord, so many of your children find themselves coveting each other. Please give us a greater understanding of your word so that we will work hard for what we need instead of being covetous. Help us reflect each day on what is right. Without your word, we will find ourselves going in the wrong direction. You said in 1 John 1:9, "If we confess our sins, he is faithful and just to forgive us our sins and to cleanse us from all unrighteousness." The sin of covetousness cause many problems in our society.

Thank you, Lord, for setting the right standard in your word to guide in this universe. If we walk by faith and read your word daily, we will be able to live a greater life until you come again. Amen.

Scripture reading: Exod. 20:17, 1 Cor. 12:31, 1 Tim. 6:10

CHAPTER 93

Prayer to Be Silent and Wait on God

Most gracious Lord, we thank you for wisdom and understanding. Grant us the ability to learn how to be silent and wait on you for all that we need. Sometimes we are afraid to be silent, but if we remain still and listen for your voice, we will be more successful in our lives. If we keep running without direction, we will find ourselves lost without hope. Isaiah 40:31 says, "But they that wait upon the Lord shall renew their strength." In you, Lord, there is no failure. Joy, peace, and love can be found in your word. Keep us humble as we wait silently on your directions each and every day.

Thank you, dear Lord, for all you have given to us in this world. Help us wait on you as long as we live. Amen.

Scripture reading: Ps. 23:2, Ps. 46:10, Ps. 37:7, Isa. 40:31, Lam. 3:26, Mark 4:39, Rom. 8:25, 1 Thess. 1:10

CHAPTER 94

Prayer Not to Bow Down to Graven Images

Precious Lord, we thank you for your word that you have given us as a road map to live by here on earth. Your word is truth and life, oh, Lord. Help us not to bow down and worship any graven images. Daniel left us an example in Daniel 3:1–30 when he and his brethren refused to bow down and worship King Nebuchadnezzar. We are so grateful for your faithful servant who showed us the way and showed us how to stand firm in your word. You prayed on your knees to your heavenly Father to forgive us of our sins. Thank you, Lord, for your love and your guidance. Please bless all of your children and help us not to bow down to any graven images. Help us bow down and pray to you, oh, Lord, and you alone. You are the only hope for tomorrow. You are the unseen God who is watching over us.

We thank you, dear Lord, for giving us all we need to live in this world of sin. Amen.

Scripture reading: Dan.3:1–30

CHAPTER 95

Prayer to Be Born Again

Dear Lord, we are living in a world that is full of mistrust and sin. Sometimes our lives do not seem to have any meaning, but your word makes perfect sense at all times. John 3:3–7 sums up your word to the great ruler who came to seek guidance from you. You told Nicodemus, "Ye must be born again.". You showed Nicodemus love and humility instead of focusing on his sinful life. You taught him that he needed the Holy Spirit to live a righteous life. This is love that only you can give to a dying world. Give us wisdom to understand that we must seek to be filled with your Holy Spirit to be born again. We cannot enter into our mother's womb and be born again. That was Nicodemus's statement. When his view was earthly, you showed him the Spirit birth instead of being born in the flesh. Your Spirit speaks life, peace, and love in the believer's ears. Thank you, dear Lord, for teaching us what really matters while living here in this world. Please help us speak in love and walk in purity as born-again children must do. You are coming back for blood-washed saints who are filled with your Holy Spirit, and then and only then will we truly know that we are born again.

Thank you, dear Lord, for hearing and answering our prayer. Amen.

Scripture reading: Isa. 9:6, Matt. 2:2, Luke 2:11, John 3:17, I John 4:7, 1 John 5:4

CHAPTER 96
Prayer to Know Jesus More

As we awake from our sleep, our minds sometimes wonder what kind of day we will have. Help us know who you are, dear Lord. We need to know you more and more each day. If we don't know your voice, then we will follow the enemy of our soul into hell. Your word declares in Job 19:25, "For I know my redeemer liveth and that he shall stand at the latter day upon the earth.". Job was in distress, but he never gave up because he knew who you were. Your children need that same kind of commitment to know your word and to stay in your word by reading and sharing with each other every day. When we know you, dear Lord, we will show love and compassion to those who are in need. Today, dear Lord, we pray that you will send the Holy Spirit to guide us as we seek to know you more and more. We are not able to do anything unless you guide us every day of our lives.

Thank you, dear Lord, for answering this prayer to know you more. Amen.

Scripture reading: Job 19:25, Ps. 46:10, Jer. 17:9, Matt. 6:3, Matt. 25:12, John 10:4, Rev. 2:2

CHAPTER 97
Prayer Not to Complain

Heavenly Father, you made man in your own image. Help us, dear Lord, to look to the cross and find comfort through the blood that flowed from your side. Sometimes we complain far too much about our circumstances instead of turning them over to you. We can do more by praying and reading your word each day than we can by complaining about things we cannot change. We complain when it rains, when it's hot, when it's cold, and even when it's dry. You are the only source of our joy. If we walk by faith, we will complain less. Help us number our days on earth, and help us, dear Lord, give you all our burdens because you are our burden bearer. In Psalm 37:7, King David said, "Rest in the Lord and wait patiently for him." . No matter how much we complain, the sun will rise in the East and set in the West because you have planned it from the beginning of time. We need your constant abiding love to not complain.

Thank you, dear Lord, for blessing us with the will to refrain from complaining unnecessarily. Amen.

Scripture reading: Ps. 37:7, Isa. 40:31

CHAPTER 98

Prayer for Contentment

Father God, we live and walk because you breathed the breath of life into our nostrils and we became living souls. You are precious and loving in all your ways. You are our helper in all we do. Without you, we cannot move one finger, we cannot speak, we cannot see, and we are totally dependent on you. Help us to be content with what we have. To those to whom much is given, much is required. You give different gifts to your children. Help us to be content with the gifts you have given and walk according to your will and your ways. Some of us refuse to be content with what we have. We work too hard, and our family life suffers because of stress and anxiety. This is not what you want for your children. God, please speak to the hearts of men and women so that we will know that you alone can solve all our problems. Please comfort our hearts in love, dear Lord, and help us pray and seek total commitment to your word. When we are content, we will have joy and peace with one another.

Thank you, dear Lord, for blessing us with total contentment. Amen.

Scripture reading: Phil. 4:7, 1 Tim 6:6, Heb. 13:5

CHAPTER 99

Prayer for God's Blessings

Dear Heavenly Father, we thank you for a new day. In spite of the weather, help us give thanks for all your blessings that you have bestowed upon us. We need your blessings each and every day to have a victorious life. Blessings come to those who seek guidance and wisdom from above. Your servant, King David, reminds us in Psalm 103:3 that "you forgiveth our iniquities and you healeth all our diseases.". Without your blessings, we will all perish without hope. Dear Lord, give us peace and joy as we wait for your abundant blessings in our lives. Help us remember to thank you each and every day for your loving-kindness and your tender mercies. If it were not for your love, we all would be lost. Please give us blessings so that we can share your goodness with our friends and families wherever we go.

Thank you, dear Lord, for hearing and answering this prayer in Jesus's precious name. Amen.

Scripture reading: Ps. 103:1–21, Ps. 104:1–35

CHAPTER 100

Prayer to Keep Our Feet in Your Own House

Most gracious Lord, you have given so much to your children. However, sometimes it seems that we wander into other people's homes instead of keeping our own homes clean. Help us not to be busybodies in other people's homes. You have given us feet to walk and to spread the good news. We pray that we will not fall in Satan's trap to allow our feet to go where we should not go. In 1 Timothy 5:13, Timothy warns us that "We should not wander from house to house. We should not be idle, nor be a tattler and speak things that we ought not to." . Please keep our hearts grounded so that we will read and share your word each and every day. When we walk, help us walk only where you would have us walk. Keep our feet secure as we travel each day, sharing your precious words.

Thank you, dear Lord, for hearing this prayer. Amen.

Scripture reading: Ps. 8:6, Ps. 116:8, Ps. 119:105, Prov. 1:16, Luke 8:35, Eph. 1:22, Eph. 6:15, 1 Tim 5:1–14

CHAPTER 101

Prayer to Be Good Housekeepers

eavenly Father, in John 14:2, you said, "In my father's house are many mansions; if it were not so, I would have told you. I go to prepare a place for you." . While we are living here on earth, Lord, please help us to be good housekeepers with the provision you have given us. A good housekeeper will read your word and seek guidance to care for his or her family. Help each housekeeper build on the strength you have given in your word each day. Without your blessings, one cannot do well here on earth. Dear Lord, we need your wisdom to raise our children in a loving way. Help all house-keepers create an atmosphere of joy, peace, and love in their homes. Please continue to watch over all housekeepers around the world.

Thank you, dear Lord, for hearing and answering this prayer in Jesus's name. Amen.

Scripture reading: Prov. 19:14, Mark 3:25, Luke 6:48, John 14:2, Acts 2:26, 2 Cor. 5:1, 1 Tim. 5:8

CHAPTER 102

Prayer to Set Our Affection on Things Above

Dear Lord, without your direction, we will not be able to keep our minds on things above. We need your constant guidance to live a Christian life here on earth. Life is not worth living if you don't control our lives. If we forget to give you praise, then we will be like a ship without a sail. Keep our hearts, minds, and souls in balance with your word. Help us set our affection on things that will bring us peace, joy, and love. Remind us that we are made from dust and we will return to dust. The only thing that can make us worthy is to turn our lives completely over to your loving hands. No one can give us peace like you can, dear Lord. In Colossians 3:2, Paul wrote, "Set your affection on things above, not on things on the earth.". Each day we need to spend time reading and sharing your word with each other so that you can be glorified. All glory and praise belong to you because you paid it all on Calvary for our sins.

Thank you, dear Lord, for hearing and answering this prayer in Jesus's name. Amen.

Scripture reading: Rom. 12:10, Gal. 5:24, Col. 3:2

CHAPTER 103

Prayer to Make It in the First Resurrection

Most Heavenly Father, so many of us are terrified about dying. We are not comfortable talking with our families and loved ones about leaving this world. Please guide us with your loving-kindness and tender mercies to face the end of our lives when you call us home. Help your children read your word and find comfort each and every day as we make preparation for our heavenly home. Paul wrote in 1 Thessalonians 4:16, "For the Lord himself shall descend from Heaven with a shout, with the voice of the archangel, and the dead in Christ shall rise first.". We must be ready to make it in the first resurrection, and only the faithful few will make it. Help your children to be ready for this great move. If we don't prepare ourselves, we will be in utter darkness. Dear Lord, you are the light of the world. Help us walk in the light so that we will be ready to meet you when you call us home to glory.

Thank you, dear Lord, for hearing and answering this prayer in Jesus's name. Amen.

Scripture reading: 1 Thess. 4:13–18

CHAPTER 104
Prayer to Use Our Time Wisely

Dear Lord, you have always been conscious of time. You made the world in six days and rested on the seventh day. You made day and night. You certainly have planned this great universe wisely. Help your children use our time wisely while living here on earth. There are so many of us who forget to thank you for the day and night that you have given. . Please help us take the time to look to the hills from whence our help comes. Help us to be thankful each day for the air we breathe. Remind us that you send the rain and sunshine as we live here on earth. Time is running out for so many of us. Disease has taken over our bodies, and we are left without hope. Time is shorter than we think, so please help us live in harmony with each other and spend each and every day wisely.

Thank you, dear Lord, for hearing and answering this prayer. Amen.

Scripture reading: Ps. 89:47, Hos. 10:12, Rom. 13:11, 1 Cor. 7:29, Eph. 5:16

CHAPTER 105
Prayer to Be Honest

Dear Lord, we are faced with so many problems in our daily lives that we sometimes fail to be honest in our doings. Help us to be mindful that being honest is a godly standard for living a good Christian life. Paul encouraged the Philippian brethren to be honest in their doings. Philippians 4:8 chronicles how so many lives were destroyed because people failed to do what was right. Please help us guide our children to practice honesty each and every day. Please remind our government and all leaders around the world that they must be honest with each and every person they serve. When we practice honesty, we will find our lives richer and happier each and every day. Honesty should be a benchmark for all people around the world.

Thank you, dear Lord, for hearing and answering this prayer. Amen.

Scripture reading: Acts 6:3, Rom. 12:17, Rom. 13:13, 2 Cor. 8:21, Phil. 4:8

CHAPTER 106
Prayer for the Sick and Afflicted

Dear Lord, sickness and affliction have always been around us since the fall of man. Sin has brought sickness on mankind. Without your healing power, we cannot make it here on earth. Your healing power is necessary for us to avoid sickness and afflictions in our bodies. We are reminded that you still hear and answer prayers, just as you did in 2 Kings 20:1–2, when Hezekiah called on you to restore his health. We need to have a heavenly connection at all times so that we can seek divine intervention for all our sickness, which comes from sin and disobedience. Please restore the joy of our salvation so that we can live a holy life free from sin. We pray for good health in all our days while living here on earth. Your word declares in 3 John 2, "Beloved, I wish above all things that thou mayest prosper and be in health, even as they soul prospereth."

We thank you, dear Lord, for hearing and answering our prayers in Jesus's name. Amen.

Scripture reading: 2 Kings 20: 1–2, 2 Chr. 32:24, Matt. 8:14, Mark 1:30, John 11:1, Acts 9:37, 3 John __:2

CHAPTER 107

Prayer for the Fowl of the Air

Most gracious Lord, loving and kind, we thank you for all that you have done in our lives. We thank you for the fowl of the air and all living things here on earth. You have made the fowl of the air to give you glory. When we look up into the skies and see the birds flying, we are reminded that you have a plan for even the fowl of the air. The fowl of the air have a purpose here on earth. When we lose animals, you have made special fowl to remove their carcasses. Yes, Lord, you have planned this universe with your children in mind. Without the fowl of the air, which exist to remove dead carcasses, we would not be able to enjoy the splendor of earth. So we thank you for this special gift that you have given us.

Thank you, dear Lord, for all your blessings. Amen.

Scripture reading: Gen. 1:20–28, Matt. 24:28

CHAPTER 108

Prayer for All the Beautiful Flowers

Heavenly Father, we thank you for the beautiful gift of flowers. Flowers remind us of your love for mankind. When you created the earth, it pleased you to sow seeds of love in each plant. You cared for even the lilies of the field. Flowers represent love that only a loving God could have created. Each and every day when the sun comes up, we are reminded that the sunshine helps each flower bloom more radiantly. We thank you, Lord, for every flower that blooms. Even the bees rejoice when the flowers bloom. You made flowers to comfort lonely hearts. Each and every day, flowers bring joy and peace to those who are sick and lonely. Our land is more beautiful because you have created beautiful flowers all around the world.

We truly thank you for every flower that blooms. Amen.

Scripture reading: Isa. 40:6

CHAPTER 109
Prayer for Jesus's Return

recious Lord, you instructed your disciples in Matthew 24 to watch, pray, and carry out your teaching here on earth. Without your heavenly guidance, we cannot fulfill this great promise you have given us. We are living in a world that has rejected some of your teachings. However, your word declares in Matthew 24:22, "Except those days should be shortened, there should no flesh be saved: but for the elect's sake, those days shall be shortened.". In spite of confusion and some disappointments here on earth, we who are believers will carry on until you come. Certainly we can see that most of your teachings have been fulfilled. Help your children keep working, watching, and praying until you come. Every day we can see the signs of the times. The people of the world are seeking fulfillment in the wrong places. We need your everlasting peace so that we can be ready when you come. Remember us, dear Lord, as we journey here below. John wrote in Revelation 22:20, "Even so, come quickly Lord Jesus.".

We thank you, dear Lord, for hearing and answering our prayer in Jesus's name. Amen.

Scripture reading: Isa. 35:10, Matt. 10:32–42, Matt. 24:30–51, Rev. 4: 8–11

CHAPTER 110

Prayer for the Redeemer

Dear Lord, each time the word "redeem" is spoken, it helps us to remember Calvary. Paul wrote in Galatians 3:13, "Christ has redeemed us from the curse of the law, being made a curse for us: 'for it is written, cursed is everyone that hangeth on a tree.'". Without Calvary, we all would be lost. You have paid a debt that we cannot pay. You paid it in full with your loving, outstretched hands; you have paid with your life so that we could be redeemed from our sins. Only a loving God who cares for his children could sustain the beating and pain that you felt when you were hung on the cross. May your children find comfort in your words each day. The only thing you require of us is to live a life free from sin. Help us, dear Lord, look to the heavens, from which our help comes. We are ever mindful of all you have done for us. King David wrote in Psalm 103:4–5, "Who redeemeth thy life from destruction; who crowneth thee with loving-kindness and tender mercies; who satisfieth thy mouth with good things; so that thy youth is renewed like the eaglets."

Thank you, dear Lord, for redemption. Amen.

Scripture reading: Ps. 44:26, Ps. 49:15, Ps. 103:4-5, Ps. 107:2, Gal. 3:13

About The Author

Audrey Athaline Addi-McNeil was born in Jamaica, West Indies, to the late Harold and Martha Rubie, where she grew up in the Church of God. When she was a young girl, prayers were always a part of her life, and they remain so to this day. Her mother always taught her and her siblings to pray both in the mornings and at night, and they knelt beside her as she prayed. The Bible was an essential part of the Rubie family's prayers. As a result of this nurturing, today Audrey's life is peaceful because she can always go to God and seek His word as often as she feels the need. When she is down and doesn't know what to do, she calls on the name of Jesus, and He always gives her comfort and joy.

Audrey was a graduate of Jericho Primary School in Hanover and Lucea School of Home Economics prior to coming to the United States. She loves cooking, sewing, interior decorating, and gardening. In 1967, Audrey migrated to the United States to work and study. She graduated from Housatonic Community College in Bridgeport, Connecticut, with an associate degree in Urban Studies. She also attended the University of Bridgeport for two years and the St. Vincent School of Nursing. She is a licensed practical nurse.

In 1989, Audrey took a course in World Religion at Sacred Heart University in Fairfield, Connecticut. She worked for eight and a half years at Hallbrooke Psychiatric Hospital in Westport, Connecticut, and for fifteen years in the Jewish Home for the Elderly in Fairfield, Connecticut. She also worked for twenty years at St. Vincent Medical Center in Bridgeport, Connecticut. Throughout those years, prayers were an integral part of her daily routine.

One of Audrey's favorite past times is reading her bible. All scripture references are from the King James Version.

Audrey hopes everyone who reads *Life-Changing Prayers* will find comfort and peace in their lives on a daily basis.

Made in the USA
Charleston, SC
03 April 2013